BARCELONA

by David J. Clarke

Book design by Kate Liestman
Cover design by Kate Liestman

Photographs ©: Gongora/NurPhoto/AP Images, cover; David Ramos/Getty Images Sport/Getty Images, 5, 8, 25; Alex Caparros/Getty Images Sport/ Getty Images, 7; Shutterstock Images, 11; Jacques Demarthon/AFP/Getty Images, 13; Keystone/Hulton Archive/Getty Images, 15; Gianni Ferrari/ Cover/Getty Images, 17; Denis Doyle/AP Images, 19; Mark Leech/Offside/ Getty Images, 21; Getty Images Sport/Getty Images, 23; Fran Santiago/ Getty Images Sport/Getty Images, 27; Quality Sport Images/Getty Images Sport/Getty Images, 29

Press Box Books, an imprint of Press Room Editions.

ISBN
978-1-63494-956-9 (library bound)
978-1-63494-970-5 (paperback)
979-8-89469-001-8 (epub)
978-1-63494-984-2 (hosted ebook)

Library of Congress Control Number: 2024911405

Distributed by North Star Editions, Inc.
2297 Waters Drive
Mendota Heights, MN 55120
www.northstareditions.com

Printed in the United States of America
012025

ABOUT THE AUTHOR

David J. Clarke is a freelance sportswriter. Originally from Helena, Montana, he now lives in Savannah, Georgia.

TABLE OF CONTENTS

CHAPTER 1

A NEW GENERATION

Things didn't look good for Barcelona at the start of the 2022–23 season. The famous soccer club was struggling for money. Many of its best players had left in recent years. That included superstar Lionel Messi. A new group of young talent had arrived. But almost no one expected Barça to win Spain's famous La Liga title.

Pedri debuted for Barcelona when he was 17.

The team didn't have much experience. However, Barcelona did have a beloved manager to lead the way. Xavi Hernández had been a star midfielder for Barcelona in the 2000s and 2010s. He proved to be a good manager, too. His team stayed on top of the standings for most of the season. With five games to go, Barcelona played local rival Espanyol on the road. If Barça won, it would clinch the league title.

One of Barcelona's young stars got the game off to a great start. In the 11th minute, left back Alejandro Balde beat his man on the wing. The 18-year-old whipped a cross into the penalty area. Superstar striker Robert Lewandowski tapped it in for a 1–0 lead.

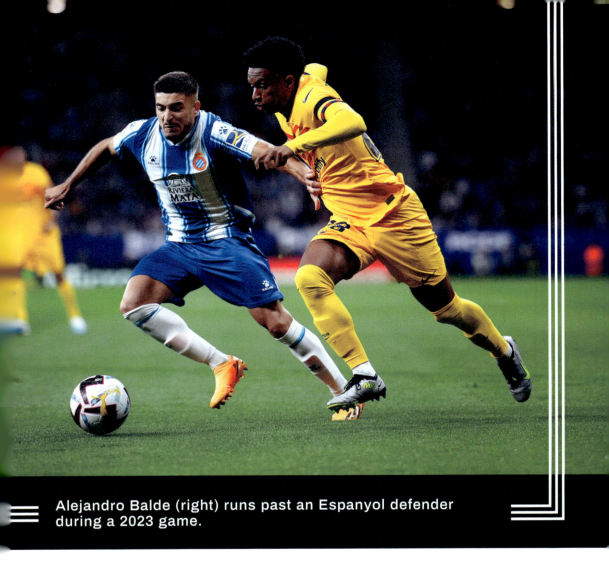

Alejandro Balde (right) runs past an Espanyol defender during a 2023 game.

Nine minutes later, Balde scored from close range. The cross came from 19-year-old midfielder Pedri. Lewandowski scored again in the 40th minute to make it 3–0. Then defender Jules Koundé added a

Barcelona players run onto the field to celebrate winning the 2022–23 La Liga title.

goal early in the second half. The title was within reach for Barcelona.

Espanyol scored two goals late in the game. But it didn't matter. The 4–2 win was enough to seal the championship for

Barcelona. This was the 27th time the club had won Spain's top league. And it may have been the most surprising championship in the team's long history. Barcelona still had financial problems to sort out. But the team's fans weren't worried about those issues. They were too busy celebrating their beloved team's return to the top.

A QUICK ESCAPE

After defeating Espanyol, Barcelona's players formed a circle at midfield. They danced there to celebrate their title. Espanyol fans were offended by the Barcelona players' actions. Some of them charged the field. Barcelona's players quickly escaped into the locker room to finish their celebration.

CHAPTER 2

CATALONIA'S CLUB

In 1898, Joan Gamper moved from Switzerland to Barcelona, Spain. Gamper loved sports. A year later, he gathered a group of fellow soccer players. They founded FC Barcelona. It was an amateur team at first. The club didn't become professional until 1926. Three years later, Barcelona helped start La Liga. That is still

With a population of 1.6 million people, Barcelona is Spain's second-largest city.

Spain's top soccer league. Barcelona became its first champion.

Barcelona is in a region of Spain called Catalonia. Many people there want the region to be its own country. The soccer team soon became a symbol of pride for the region. The team logo even shows the Catalan flag.

That pride often caused problems for the team. This was especially true when Spain began fighting a civil war in 1936. When the war ended in 1939, a new government took over in Spain. Dictator Francisco Franco became the country's leader. He banned symbols and ideas he did not agree with. That included the Catalan flag.

ATALONIA IS NOT SPAIN

During a home game in 2002, Barcelona fans display a banner in support of Catalonia becoming its own country.

Spain's government was based in the country's capital city, Madrid. That city was home to Real Madrid. Barcelona and Real Madrid had long been rivals. After Franco took over, the rivalry became even more heated. Barcelona fans often thought that Real Madrid got unfair advantages.

Barcelona still played well on the field. In 1950, the club hired manager Ferdinand Daučík. His teams won La Liga twice in four years. He also led Barcelona to three Copa del Rey titles. That is Spain's top cup competition.

Daučík left in 1954. Forward Luis Suárez kept the team humming. The star

CHANGES UNDER FRANCO

After Francisco Franco took power, Barcelona had to make many changes. For example, it had to remove the Catalan flag from its logo. The club even had to change its name. Since its founding, it had been called Fútbol Club Barcelona. But Franco didn't think that was Spanish enough. So, the club had to be called Club de Fútbol Barcelona until Franco's death in 1975.

Luis Suárez scored 141 goals in 253 games for Barcelona.

scored 141 goals for Barcelona from 1955 to 1961. In 1960, he was named the best player in Europe. After Suárez left, Barcelona fell off. The club didn't win another La Liga title in the 1960s. The bad times wouldn't last, though. Soon, a superstar would arrive and change Barcelona forever.

CHAPTER 3

TOTAL FOOTBALL

Dutch forward Johan Cruyff was one of the world's best players in the 1960s and 1970s. He helped create a new style of play called "Total Football." In 1973, Cruyff joined Barcelona. The team played Total Football. The strategy called for players to move all over the field. They often changed places with one another. Everyone

Johan Cruyff scored 20 goals for Barcelona during his first season with the club.

had to pass well. They also had to play multiple positions. This strategy helped the team keep the ball. Fans loved the club's exciting new style. And Cruyff soon led Barcelona back to the top. Barça won La Liga in 1973–74. That win was the team's first championship in 14 years.

Cruyff left Barcelona as a player in 1978. A decade later, he returned as manager. Soon, Barça turned into a machine. Starting in 1991, the club won La Liga four years in a row. The club featured many star players. They were called the "Dream Team." Forward Hristo Stoichkov could score goals with ease. Sweeper Ronald Koeman led the defense. Josep "Pep" Guardiola was a rising star.

Hristo Stoichkov scored 122 goals in 262 games for Barcelona.

The midfielder had come through the team's famous academy.

In 1991–92, Barcelona reached the final of the European Cup. Today, that tournament is called the Champions

League. Barcelona created many scoring chances in the final. But the game went to extra time tied 0–0. In the 112th minute, Barça received a free kick 30 yards from goal. Koeman stepped up to take it. He blasted a low shot into the corner of the net. Barcelona held on to win and claim its first European title.

LA MASIA

In 1979, Barcelona turned an old farmhouse into a camp for youth players. The camp became known as *La Masia* (The Farmhouse). Before long, it was known as one of the best youth academies in world soccer. Superstars such as Pep Guardiola, Lionel Messi, Xavi Hernández, and Andrés Iniesta all lived at La Masia as young players.

Ronald Koeman (far right) celebrates his game-winning goal during the 1992 European Cup final.

Cruyff left Barcelona in 1996. He had won 11 trophies. No manager had won more with the club. However, one of his own players would soon top that total.

CHAPTER 4

TIKI-TAKA

In the summer of 2008, Barcelona hired Pep Guardiola as its manager. He took over a strong team. In the early 2000s, Barcelona and Real Madrid were the two best teams in Spain. However, Guardiola soon put Barcelona far ahead of its rival. Barcelona won La Liga in his first season. The club also won the Copa del Rey and the

Barcelona won 14 trophies when Pep Guardiola (top center) managed the team.

Champions League that year. Those wins completed a treble. That is when a team wins three major competitions in one season.

Barcelona continued to roll after that. In 2009–10, the team lost only one La Liga match. The next season, Barça lost only twice. Barcelona won the league again in 2010–11.

SIX FOR SIX

In 2009, Barcelona won La Liga and the Copa del Rey. It also won the Champions League. In August, Barcelona added the Club World Cup, the Spanish Super Cup, and the European Super Cup. It was the first time any European club team had won six titles in one calendar year.

Starting with the 2008–09 season, Lionel Messi scored at least 30 goals every year for 13 straight seasons with Barcelona.

Guardiola's teams played lots of quick, short passes. The style was called "tiki-taka." Barcelona featured many talented players. Midfielders Xavi Hernández and Andrés Iniesta were two of the best players in the world. But no player could match Lionel Messi.

Opponents couldn't stop the speedy forward. In 2011–12, Messi set a La Liga record by scoring 50 times.

Guardiola left after that season. Messi didn't slow down, though. In 2014–15, he led Barcelona to another treble. Barça went on to win four La Liga titles in five years. Messi didn't do it alone. Neymar and Luis Suárez helped form a lethal attacking line.

Barcelona enjoyed success on the field. But off the field, problems loomed. The club had spent big on players. It no longer had the money for those huge salaries. Many stars left the club. In 2021, Messi moved on, too. He had been at the club for 17 years.

Robert Lewandowski scored a team-high 33 goals during the 2022–23 season for Barcelona.

Barcelona started to rebuild with young players. Former star Xavi Hernández returned to manage the club. He led the team to a league championship in 2022–23. That title was Barcelona's first in four years. Barça finished second the next season. After that result, the club fired Xavi. Fans hoped it wouldn't be long before the club got back to its winning ways.

SUPERSTAR PROFILE

LIONEL MESSI

From a young age, Lionel Messi was a soccer prodigy in Argentina. His only problem was his lack of size. Messi needed daily hormone treatments to grow.

Barcelona wanted Messi badly. When he was 13, the club agreed to pay for his treatments. Within three years, Messi started playing for Barcelona's first team. At the time, he was the club's youngest ever player. Messi became a world superstar with Barça. He grew to be only 5-foot-7 (170 cm). But he didn't need height. Messi could dribble past defenders with his quick feet. And he finished off his runs with accurate shots. Many soccer fans consider him the best player in the sport's history.

Messi stayed at Barcelona through the 2020–21 season. In 778 appearances, he scored 672 goals. The Ballon d'Or is awarded to the best player in the world each season. Messi won the trophy seven times in his Barcelona career.

Lionel Messi helped Barcelona win 35 trophies during his 17 seasons with the club.

QUICK STATS

BARCELONA

Founded: 1899

Home stadium: Camp Nou

La Liga titles: 27

European Cup/Champions League titles: 5

Copa del Rey titles: 31

Key managers:

- Ferdinand Daučík (1950–54): 2 La Liga titles, 3 Copa del Rey titles
- Johan Cruyff (1988–96): 4 La Liga titles, 1 European Cup title, 1 Copa del Rey title
- Pep Guardiola (2008–12): 3 La Liga titles, 2 Champions League titles, 2 Copa del Rey titles

Most career appearances: Lionel Messi (778)

Most career goals: Lionel Messi (672)

Stats are accurate through the 2023–24 season.

GLOSSARY

academy
A program set up by a professional soccer club to develop young players.

amateur
Having to do with players who are not paid.

dictator
A leader with absolute power, especially one who uses that power in a cruel way.

extra time
Two 15-minute halves that take place if a knockout game is tied after 90 minutes of play.

penalty area
The 18-yard box in front of the goal where a player is granted a penalty kick if he or she is fouled.

prodigy
A young person with exceptional skill.

professional
Made up of people who are paid to do something as a job.

rival
An opposing player or team that brings out the greatest emotion from fans and players.

TO LEARN MORE

Hewson, Anthony K. *GOATs of Soccer*. North Mankato, MN: Abdo Publishing, 2022.

McDougall, Chrös. *The Best Rivalries of World Soccer*. Minneapolis: Abdo Publishing, 2024.

Moon, Derek. *Lionel Messi: Soccer Star*. Mendota Heights, MN: Focus Readers, 2023.

MORE INFORMATION

To learn more about Barcelona, go to **pressboxbooks.com/AllAccess**. These links are routinely monitored and updated to provide the most current information available.

INDEX